Real Daughter

Real Daughter

Lynn Otto

2017 Selection
First Book Award

Unicorn Press   Greensboro

First printing

Paper   ISBN 978-0-87775-032-1
Cloth   ISBN 978-0-87775-033-8

COVER IMAGE. "Knit Process V" by
Carol MacDonald. Photograph
courtesy of Andy Duback.

∞

This book is printed on Mohawk Via,
which is acid-free and meets ANSI
standards for archival permanence.

Unicorn Press
Post Office Box 5523
Greensboro, NC 27435
unicorn-press.org

Distributed to the trade
by Small Press Distribution
of Berkeley, California

For Joey, Lauren, and April, with love

Real Daughter

2

3

Real Daughter

I

Marcescence

The beeches' light brown leaves in horizontal layers
like my mother's tiered serving trays
artfully placed in the winter forest and here we are,
in another stupid tree poem, this one
about the difficulty of letting go of something already dead.

Such a fancy word for it when it comes to trees:
marcescence. You could name a daughter that.
Unlike *fury*. Unlike *grief*.

Like the beeches, I'm slow to harden my cells,
allow *abscission*, another elegant arboreal term,
those tidy partings between twig and withered leaf,
or the calm release of ripe fruit.

Consider the clean white spaces
between each layer of a family tree.
It isn't like that at all.

Family Tree

In the beginning
we just rested in its shade.
My mother braided and rebraided my hair
and I did the same for my daughter.

Sometimes we let down my mother's hair,
brushed and braided it with ours.
We sat close together and admired the rope we had made,
laughed about our entanglement.

So you understand
when my mother ate the fruit,
we ate it too. We agreed
it was delicious.

Later we were sick together.
Later, my mother cut her hair because she was too weak to hold up its heaviness.
My daughter cut her hair because I loved it.
I cut mine because it kept catching in the branches.

Still with My Mother

A doe gave birth in the yard below.
So still with my mother at the window,

I spoke low of what we both could see—look, look.
From holding myself motionless, an ache

came up my legs and back. Was it so long?
The mother nudged and nursed the just-born fawn

and then ignored it, turned away and strained
until a second tumbled to the ground—

she licked it clean. Then both came to her sides,
and when she walked, they followed her to nearby woods.

How thin, how fine, the fawns and their mother.
They all knew what to do, and have I ever?

In This Green Green So Blue

In this green green,
a hundred shades, turning
pancakes on the Coleman stove,
fewer than last year,
fewer than the mother in site 22,
visible through vine maples and huckleberries,
spring-green screen
too thin.

Yesterday, like the flicker overhead she fussed
poor directions to her husband
as he backed a trailer between the ferns and firs and alders
without consequence.

Since then, her children and their young spouses,
as if ordered from a catalog,
have arrived.

They laugh together, beautiful
under the pale green streamers of moss,
and smile at their ordinary mother,
who sings and sets
the rough wood table for ten.

Revision

Let's unhook ten months from the nail in the wall,
let fall again the pages of sad days.

I'll do them over.

This time, I will leave
the cigarettes in my daughter's purse.

This time, I will take
up smoking.

Then she will take
a different path,

one that's not
called leaving.

The Douglas Fir Leans Toward
the House and I Pretend It Doesn't

For who can see
a heart turning?

The angle of the jaw.
The ratio of silence.
Should I have measured?

On Sunday, I'll call my mother.
All the answers will be *Fine*.

She used to say a stitch in time saves nine—
it's what I told my daughter.

We applied this
only to mending.

Those White Amish Bonnets

If we wore white bonnets
it would have been obvious
my daughter took hers off.
I'd know when.
I'd have looked for it in the trash.
Washed it and saved it.
Or maybe found it in her pocket.

We Move to Morton Street

My husband thinks of salt, the girl with the umbrella,
a sunny yellow dress. I think of death,

la mort. When it rains, it pours.
When it stops, we pull out the overgrown shrubs,

contemplate the empty beds for months, undecided. Not roses
because deer come up from the ravine. They browse

the neighborhood, nibbling off the blooms with their black lips,
dwarfing the plastic deer next door, who eat nothing.

Only in that chain-linked yard the roses thrive
and three fat Chihuahuas, who nonchalantly blink

until you touch the gate. The deer step past,
past the duplex in its tangle of blackberries,

where weeds wave from the back of a pickup on blocks
and grocery ads turn to pulp in their plastic bags,

though someone lives there on the left side. Black shirt, black pants,
he comes and goes in a black Camaro. No roses

and none at the yellow house, where no one lives
except when the daughter returns to visit her dead parents'

things. Sits on the couch she grew up with, drinks
from the same cups from the same cupboard.

In the grey house, the guy tries to forget
he ran over a kid in the crosswalk. His wife hollers

for help when he gets out of hand, and someone calls 9-1-1
and the deer spook down the street. At the end of the block,

the divorcée. Her flower beds collect cigarette butts
while she strokes the cat that hangs around.

Her son will wreck the car and she knows it.

Nobody Knew Them at the Blue Note Grill

So even though nobody else was dancing,
they danced, and she felt free to dance wildly,
or more precisely largely, taking up space, plenty of it,
but after two songs he sat, just

too tired or the blues got his mind.
But she asked anyway,
each song, and especially
the slow ones. Did he mind

she said yes to the Willie Nelson wannabe
who offered himself? She felt all
hinges out of oil, didn't want to
smile at the man, and his moves

were not familiar moves, and how
can a married woman slow-dance
with somebody else on Valentine's Day
and like it. They drove

home, and whatever had been
holding them together seemed
suddenly broken, as when a bolt
goes missing and the parts shift

away from each other
or clang or scrape,
abrading each other with the grit
that's come between them.

Dry Dock

After the shakes were over he built ships
in the best of the empty bottles.

She didn't mind the first few. Admiring
people said how did he ever.

She'd say with a chopstick and a very long tweezer.
But the growing fleet

went nowhere. Masts and rigging like bird bones
but safe in there.

The sails wouldn't really billow
even if she uncorked a bottle and blew in it.

Next-to-invisible
dots of glue held everything. She thought

about the inaccessible,
places they used to go, what it would take

to get in or get out,
and whether she would want to.

Gap

All along the street, there are such great gaps between the front yards
and the glossy magazine photographs that must have inspired
the effort, which is still faintly visible among the weeds.
                                   Or between the past,
when days held more hours, and now, when we still want
the flowers our mothers lived for.
                                   Roses, and rosemary,
my mother chose, and a host of others, their colors
harmonious, the beds sharp-edged, the grass
and sidewalk also kept separate.
Later, sick, she bought
more time with a breathing machine,
parked her wheelchair in the sun;
and somewhere between
duty and love,
            I tended her
while my roses grew more spare.
Some grub lived there.

Instructions in Case of Interruptive Insomnia

Brown leather purses

carports you have known

garages if you've never seen a carport

children's books
no, scratch that one

hardware stores will do

or flowers

feathers

no
the small grey feathers stuck to the window this morning

you don't want dead birds in your bed
at 2 a.m. when you toss and fret about your son
your daughter

your diminishing mother and father

think instead of brown purses

the tooled Mexican handbags for sale at the state fair

the flowers and birds in bas relief

birds again
think

the soft suede bags with fringes

the purse your aunt let you rummage through during church

the Gumby key chain

the tiny address book

the compact of pressed powder with its dusty mirror

if this brings your mother to mind, skip it

go on to the wallet with its various pockets

the envelope pocket for dollar bills

the accordion pocket for change

its two-pronged metal clasp

the slight resistance

the scrape

one part pushing past the other

and under the snap, the picture sleeves

or next on the list, carports/garages

unless you find them too cluttered or dirty

you can always move on

grocery stores

gas stations

the corner hardware

yes
you could go through the nail bins

common nails

box nails

finishing nails

double-headed scaffold nails

roofing nails

their large flat heads galvanized rough

let their sharp points

soothe you

if you need to

go to the next aisle

examine the paintbrushes

finger their handles

press the bristles

against your palm

pick

a soft one

the softest

so slowly

brush it over

your face

your eyelids

Now a Wheelchair, Now a Head Restraint

Did we expect the mountain to sit unchanged under its snowcap?
Inexperienced, we concluded the world was finished forming itself.
The occasional wandering river. Small erosions. So what?

So few facts. For our grandparents grew old in another country.
This is how we imagined it: they sat in rocking chairs, each day
rocking a little more slowly. White plaster walls and crocheted coverlets.

In truth we did not think of them at all. We played with Malibu Barbie
and Malibu Ken and only their clothes got wrinkled. Once a year,
we sat under our school desks for the earthquake drill. Nothing shook us.

We should have stashed some handkerchiefs to wipe her chin, should have
bought a boat and tied it to the front porch waiting.

Maytag

It can't be fixed, says my father
of the dryer, the Maytag of many years—most
of their marriage—and the protest
of my mother, who can't do laundry anymore anyway,
doesn't stop him from having it hauled away,
ordering a Kenmore.

What he means is *he* can't fix it. He has fallen
and what can a man do with a broken rib?
The third bird in two days hits the window and drops,
a rose-breasted nuthatch I place in a napkin,
but they won't touch its fine fine feathers for fear of lice.
I'm to throw it in the bay.

If my daughter were here, she would bury it in a small box,
lined with a scrap of soft cloth.
But there's no time for dead birds.
The crabs creep out sideways to clean up,
and my mother says to call the crematorium the minute she dies.
When the Maytag goes, she cries.

Omen Envy

A tuft of fur beside the road, soft brown, pink ruffle
of intestine, and down the bank,
the dead rabbit, headless.

An owl watches from the branch above.
Its lids close slowly, open slowly—
Sexy eyes, Aunt says.

Mother in her wheelchair smiles,
shivers, and her air pump begins
its piercing alarm.

The battery is fine, fine—
the air still shoves into her—
but she gasps, panics, is gasping
even after we're home, even after
we shift her tubing to the spare pump,
plugged in.
We crush white pills between spoons,
slip the powder under her tongue, then
lift her into bed, two pillows just so,
another under her calves to keep
the thin skin of her heels off the sheet

and soon she's snoring.

Some people think the owl's an omen. Somewhere
    I've read it, somewhere death's warning.
        It's not, however, on the hospice list.

Now three eagles lift over the bay.
    They circle twice then spiral off,
        each its own way.

Couldn't that mean something too?
    Or maybe the hummingbird with its frantic tongue.
        Or the blinking, red-eyed common loon.

By

I stood by her
Then I stood by

There is the innocent bystander
And the guilty bystander

Or frightened
And frightened

Doesn't Even

She works for peace,
crafts her sentences carefully
to maintain harmony. She gets
better at it with time.
Does it matter

that the scope of her efforts
is strictly domestic.
Can we argue,
given Maslow's hierarchy,
that her focus is necessary.

Does it matter this peace
turns out to be external. Paint
covering wood rot.
Makeup over
dark circles under the eyes.

As for her children,
they eventually notice and are
ungrateful.
Their disdain moves her
to reconsider:

what happens to women
who speak their mind. Angry
men frighten her
and she doesn't even
have any bruises.

One Story

Some birds here, thrushes maybe,
call all day, sounding like a cold wind
whistling through a window
barely open. How is it we each learn
one story, and every sentence ever after
sounds to us like it belongs to it?
I know this one, says the careless brain
with its one groove, a particular chain
of synapses firing fast, so practiced,
so sure the wind is cold, sure
there is no end to yearning. If only
the window were not open,
if the birds would just shut up.

Doesn't Equal

Strength, my mother wished me,
but in Dutch, *sterkte*, which I find

also means tenacity, able to hold on
(likely her intent).

To my dreams,
did she mean, or my sanity?

Or my tongue, when prudent.
Be still now, she'd say. It took

a strength that doesn't equal
power. A different meaning:

fortress. A shard-topped wall
to keep the inside safe.

I've Told You Here

White wakes of ducks,
white rings, momentary fish,
and the lake again glass.
Did I tell you she boarded the bus?

She boarded the bus.
I pointed to
its digital destination sign,
mouthed Wrong bus! Wrong bus!

But she smiled and blew me a kiss,
gave me the finger.

Had I filmed all
the temporary lines,
all the rings of all the fish
rising to kiss the surface,

and could show all
the frames at once,
the picture would be covered
in X's and O's.

But there is no record of anything
aside from what I've told you here.

Part

God, grant me ... the courage
to change the things I can ...

Concerned, my husband reminded me
of the old serenity prayer,
so I'm parting my hair on the left instead,
and I've moved to the empty chair.

Can't say my serenity's grown at all.
Perhaps I need to change more.
But now I see what my daughter saw—
instead of the wall, the door.

Reading Wendell Berry to My Parents in the Hospital,
That Distant Land Comes Close

My mother opens her eyes when I pause, so I persist
with Wheeler Catlett of Port William struggling
to fulfill his obligation to Jack Beechum, deceased.
I am sitting at her feet.

She is tilted up in the hospital bed,
her breathing mask breathing for her,
her breathing mask pressing on the painful tube in her nose
that drains her punctured stomach
while the botched operation tries to mend,

and my father in his Sunday best
sleeps on a vinyl recliner next to her.
He's spent from watching her through the night
because he will not let me take his place.
He believes he knows what she wants.

Wheeler knows what Beechum wants,
but Beechum's daughter doesn't give a damn,
she'll sell the farm to the highest bidder, to hell
with Elton and Mary Penn, who cared for her father
and the land he cared for. I want to
know what will happen,

and my mother wants to know,
and what about the house she's kept,
who will watch the bay she's loved,
and will her daughters care for their father?

Both our mouths are dry, but she can't drink.
Today they said not even ice chips.
I take a small sip. The daughter,
in a fur coat, waits near the courthouse steps.
She's giddy with her approaching freedom,
and I recognize that fantasy—who asks for complications?

The morphine is persuasive. Her eyes again close.
I want her to rest easy, and long silence might wake my father,
and I need this education,
so I keep reading aloud from my chair near their feet,
speaking Wendell Berry's words in Wheeler Catlett's mouth,
explaining what it means to succeed, to be a successor,
to be given something, to accept it.

2

Horizon

Bent low, I place
the back of my hand
on the earth.

Everything above
I hold in my palm.

Which do I feel:
the pull of earth
or the weight of heaven?

I cannot keep
the two apart.

At Six, I Felt the Sacred

The solid pew, first cool, then warm,
the shared weight of the Psalter hymnal,
the small cross embossed on its cover.

In heat of summer, window breeze.
In winter, my body's heat inside my coat,
the heavy prickle of my feet asleep.

The calluses of my father's hands,
his jacket's coarse wool, his handkerchief
knotted and folded for me, a small doll.

And my mother's gloves of soft soft leather,
the eternal circles of her buttons,
her nyloned knees

and valleyed lap where I lay my head,
her fingers stroking over my ear,
over and over, stroking my hair.

She Often Said

If it's not nice don't say it.
She was otherwise very quiet.

Four Parts Holy Water

I wanted to dip my fingers in the holy water
but my mother said it was full of germs

Always cleanliness and godliness
fighting for the front seat

And the rain fell and fell
forty days and forty more

soaking us and the neighbors
who never washed their car

Then two by two, the little plastic animals came
with fill-ups at the ARCO

My mother said no children
came with little plastic Noah

I dreamt she cried *Jesus!*
and wept when I left

What she actually said was
Did you check your windshield wiper fluid?

Otter

Rowing the dory near the dock,
I thought I saw an otter
below my oar.
Though my mother called, I paused,
loath to dock the boat and go indoors
when an otter might be near.
I dawdled. And when I walked
through the door, my mother roared about
my sloth and boxed my ears.
She made me throw away the minnows
I had caught.
So I threw them to the otter. I thought
it was an otter. It might have been
some rocks.

Spin

How have I "spun" you, mother, when I meant
to tease you out, not tease you, not mock

but untangle you, unknot,
to see what you were

made of.
Love

shakes my head
and shames me, doubts what I have said.

Extracurricular

Beyond caution, hard work, seemliness, and thrift,
my mother taught me forsythia and what it meant,
and that green was not one color.

She showed me signs to look for:
new leaves like tiny flames,
and bright bursts at conifer tips.

I learned the fairytale names
of ferns, and that a leaf showing its silver
is waiting for the wind's promised shower.

She paused, and made me pause,
for what she called the gilded hour,
when the sun sinks low enough

to shine below the long grey skies
and makes every color warm.
From her I learned the galvanic smell of rain

and the earth after a rain. To break open
a freshly picked bell pepper
and inhale something similar,

to notice the dank odor of a cold tree
and its different scent when hot. She listened
and helped me listen to pinecones ticking open,

to the forest's summer breathing,
its rattling in fall, and the various calls
of all its transitory residents.

A Piece of Knitting Pantoum

*Cast off: to remove [stitches] from a knitting
needle in such a way as to prevent unraveling*
MERRIAM-WEBSTER

Each piece, when finished, is cast off
Each stitch passes over another
Bit by bit, picked up, slipped off
A daughter is taught by her mother

Each stitch passing over some other
Makes a chain on the edge of something warm
The daughter then teaches another
The last takes the end and holds it firm

This chain on the edge of something warm
Holds onto the work of repeated rows
The last takes the end and holds it firm
How long it will hold, nobody knows

Hold fast the work of repeated rows
Bit by bit, picked up, slipped off
How long it can hold, nobody knows
Each piece is finished, cast off

Daughter through the Open Door

On the back of her left hand, where the thumb bone meets the fingers,
a half-dollar dollop of makeup, a shade paler than her skin. She dips a finger in,
daubs dots across her cheekbones, forehead, chin. Then small strokes
smooth the mask across her face, some magazine-model beauty. Yet the stranger
that appears is not her face—the makeup doesn't really change her—
it's the dollop on her hand. A technique, I think, of the women in white smocks
at makeup counters of fancier shops, where I never linger, or try another brand.
I tip the bottle to my finger. My daughter tips the bottle to her hand.

Haiku on a Daughter's Departure

Is what they say true,
that you will reap what you sow?
But spring is long gone!

When children run wild,
careless in the summer heat,
snakes watch from the shade.

I take out a leaf
and the table is shorter.
One less bowl of soup.

Her made bed stays made,
a field of snow that won't melt
until I lie there.

Comfort, Comfort Me

I have come to church with the dust of broken things in my lungs
I have come with the broken in my throat
I croak the gospel choruses
I mouth the psalms doubting

Just give me a sip of mercy
Let me hear the story of repair

I Swear

Every night I need my eyelids kissed they've worked so dang
hard staying open all day I swear my husband's lips are magic
his kisses better than used tea bags but during the day they're
too far away yap yap yapping about wampum which he says is
not Native American money honey but that's what everyone
thinks anyway in his pocket a tiny clear plastic box holds all
he has two little tubes of white shell I swear he dreams about
those beads.

One day I drove to his office with my eyes shut they hurt so
bad I swear I could only think of his lips and his secretary said
he was still in class so I asked her to take me there I could tell
she felt weird about holding my arm and I heard those history
students snicker when I said honey my eyes are so tired I need
your magic kisses and he said honey honey maybe you need
some new glasses and kissed each eyelid just right I swear if
I could I'd anoint him with wampum pour over him handfuls
and handfuls and handfuls.

French Kiss

Go ahead
I've left you
a tiny tuna salad snack
between my teeth
I know
you'd prefer chocolate
but a girl can't live on it

What Happens When Women Pray

Please indicate the reason for your return:
__It didn't fit __It's not what I ordered __It came too late

Rain falls or doesn't.
The phone rings or is silent.

Momentary hope is momentarily calming
even if the baby won't be soothed.

Prayer is credited
when the breathing improves,

when the biopsy is negative.
Otherwise:

Cancer as enlightenment.
Death as mercy.

Bargaining.
Doubt.   (Does God even like you?)

About back-seat driving:
the driver can ignore you,

take the turns too fast,
leave the main highway for some desolate pot-holed road.

Maybe you'll get home.
Maybe your children will arrive safely.

After the Flood

Among the mud-bloated cattle,
among the fattened crows discussing the landscape,
what will fill our mouths
besides our bitter tongues. Bowls
of foul air? Should we not have
prayed for rain?

Warped doors give way to rubbled rooms.
Where windows were,
stained curtains luff lakeward.
Let us kneel to consider the limits of algorithms
and whether God is good.
Surely we believed our prayers

are sifted, that right requests
would settle on God's ear like specks of gold
in a miner's pan, all worthless bits
washed out. No doubt
the sun was wanted elsewhere. Maybe
there's a balance to maintain,

a see-saw system of losses and gains.
Of course a crow
is laughing in the sycamores—
it doesn't care the foliage droops all sodden and forgetful.
And look at the ants, the competing spiders,
all the beetles still clinging to the bark.

Yoked

for Paul

How is a yoke borne? The ox and the ox—
the farmer goads the one, and it walks, so both walk—
the farmer taps the other, and it turns, so both turn—
they can't turn away from each other.

A husband and wife feel their marriage chafe.
Always the other. Often not what they'd rather:
the room too hot and too cold,
the calendar cluttered, the accounts

scrutinized, insufficient. Each body grows old.
In the distance, other possible selves,
places they might have gone if.
Behind the oxen, the earth

opens and turns, like fresh sheets turned back on the bed.
They face only the hard ground ahead,
yet they feel the resistance give.
Imagine a crop there, thriving in perfect weather—

it might or might not turn out like that—
there are countless kinds of disaster.
And the wife and the husband can turn away from each other—
this yoke is not a wooden thing—

or they can turn toward each other, and cling,
as they do some nights when they're not too tired,
to the solace of familiar skin.
Your eyes, she might say again, *are like Picasso eyes*

when we're this close. Overlapping
almond shapes, one slightly over the other.
And he might again say, *You are a strange thing,*
and stay there, his forehead touching hers.

Makeup (The Mother, the Daughter,
and the Other Daughter Speak)

ı   Lipstick

Now a Walgreens Beauty Consultant,
my daughter drops in
with wrinkle-reducing foundation,
waterproof mascara,
and lipstick in colors I've never heard of:
   All Angel, Innocence, Paradise, Peace.
I ask if there's one called Sin.
She flinches, turns away,
but I say I like Peace, which is peach and pretty subtle.
She uncaps the tube, says
   Smile,
And I know this is what she wants.
She would draw one on my face if she could.

2　*Foundation*

Sometimes, when I am stocking the shelves
or helping a customer find the right shade of blush,
I see my mother come in. She looks for me,
scanning aisles 13, 14, 15. I wave
and she waits, small, at the makeup counter,
her gray hair beautiful, her face plain.
Then I take my place behind the register
with good posture, as if she is a customer.

　　She always was, when I was small, and I ran
　　the little plastic cash register, counted the fake bills,
　　the weightless coins, with Thank you, come again!
　　And she would, smiling, in a different hat.

Your mail, she says today, not smiling, hands me a bag,
heavy and warm. Also some bread, she says,
and it doesn't seem right, but
I stow it underneath, show her
something I think she might like,
Revlon Age Defying Makeup for Dry Skin, soft beige.

She turns the bottle in her hand, strokes it,
strokes the red lid, the square glass sides,
as if she's feeling fabric or a baby's hand,
strokes it so long I reach for it, finally,
and she says she'll think about it, lets it go.

3 Shadow

I used to have
  a sister.
We shared
  this blue room,
  her side messy,
too busy
  to fold her clothes
  but she could make
  herself pretty.

I keep it
  neat now. Sometimes
I see a girl
  when I'm out with my mother.
  The girl looks
like her
  if she cut her
  hair short and bleached it
  white. It might be

her. One time
  this girl rang our doorbell.
I was alone,
  unlocked
  the door.
Movie star
  smile. Red red.
  Smelled like
  cigarettes.

She asked if I'd seen her
  green scarf
and was there anything good
  in the fridge.
  No and no,
but she took
  the last link
  of sausage, left
  grease on the towel.

I have something
  for you she said,
reached
  in her big red bag.
  Pink lip gloss.
After she left,
  I
  put some on.
  Not too much.

Edges

Grand and gilded and finely carved with leaves,
fleurs-de-lis, flowers, fruits, rows of beads,
the frame distracts from the fact
of the painting's edges. No one asks about
the unpictured sisters, the rest of the family, what lies
on either side of the green field.
No one feels the earth drop away. They lean in,
breathing on the verticals, the gold grapes,
the apples, the veined, overlapping leaves.

Letter from a Reader

Is the silent mother in your story
really your mother or
did you make her up?

And is the daughter your daughter
or some version of yourself
or someone else entirely?

Did these people ever give you
their permission to be used?

The mother who doesn't smile,
is she supposed to be God?

Or is the mother merely you
wearing makeup?

If you could write back
and explain everything
I'd feel more comfortable.

I'd give you my permission to be used
as long as you told me
exactly what I meant.

3

And After

Now the pin oak and the alder
drop their leaves, all tarnished
forks and spoons,

and their burden shows:
a broken pine cradled there.

It rests in their arms,
a confluence of angles,

festoons their lower branches
with dead needles, small bundles
dangling like rusty tinsel.

They will hold the pine while it is dying
and after. Their growth
must accommodate its weight.

Its constraint, even after it crumbles,
will mark them in the way they're bent.

Soup

When the clouds finally edged their way in,
    when they shoved summer south and stole my mother,
I chopped things small and simmered them with bones for hours,
    and a small cloud hovered over the pot.

Taste, my mother would say, when she made soup, and would slip
    a piece of carrot in my mouth, her knife close to my lips.

Over the stove, I breathed in her garden, her body
    kneeling between the rows.
So quiet there. Only the scratch of the cultivator,
    its clink against stones. If she spoke,
she spoke of carrots.
    Carrots and celery and onions.

I craved something sweeter,
    even bitter or sour, whatever was inside her,
and as her voice grew weaker,
    I leaned over her bed, waiting for revelation.

Still it was carrots, nothing of consequence,
    then only her breath, barely.

Shall I say it? Sometimes it was so bitter
    I thought she was poisoned.
I'll tell you more: if, as a child, I pouted,
    that knife would come out and threaten me:
Must I make lip soup?
    I would suck in my lips, cover my mouth with my hands.

Same Mother

Sister, if we Venn-diagram our versions,
I am jealous of your unshared crescent:

the frequent phone calls, for instance,
the ease with which you sat together,

and your grief—a simple A-line dress in blue
while I've got nothing appropriate.

Once I felt myself our mother's favorite,
made in her image, who asked for nothing.

She was silent when I took up smoking.
Silent when I married the risky boy.

My children shined me up again.
Each held her hand and mine,

and for a while we smiled over them.
And then?

Powder

My mother's leftover yellow face powder
(to balance redness, hush a blush)
whispers from behind my mirror:
of course we should keep our secrets.

Matryoshka

My mother explained nesting dolls
as mothers and daughters,
each holding the next generation inside her.

But I carry my mother
inside me, and my daughter,
she carries me.

And if it's my mother's dismay
I carry—her held tongue, her look away—
my daughter carries it too.

These identical painted smiles.
Even my grandmother's sorrows
rattle within us, her secret fears.

Mirror

There, your face in mine, mother.
Spitting image.
Say something, why don't you.

If I brush your hair?
If I brush it up from my neck?
If I brush it back from my forehead,
will you let go what furrows it?

In the old garden your feet
paced the rows. You marked them
with pine stakes, guided them with string.
Your finger drew each one, your hands
pressed down each seed.
You tended the shoots, the roots,
the quiet blooms.

Looking in your eyes, I
hear outside some robin staking claim.
Open your mouth and answer.
Say what is yours.

My Mother Doesn't Visit

my dreams. She doesn't appear
to guide me.

Even when I hover
in front of some oven unable
to call the dish done

or undone
while a crowd crowds me
inquiring, all their eyes hungry,

nothing.
No one.

Her mother stood by
the mailbox, waiting.
For what?

A letter? A ride somewhere?
She didn't tell me
if they talked.

I walk to the mailbox
every day. I wouldn't leave her
standing there.

I'd say *A cup of tea?*
and *Are you better now?*
Maybe she's waiting

for an invitation.
Yes, right,
not the drop-in type.

Okay then: Dear Mom,
How about this Tuesday,
anytime after dark?

If we lived in the right place,
I could hire a shaman.
It might cost me

a chicken
and a bag of beans, but I like the idea
of a go-between—

it would feel so good
to unfasten our lips and clear the air
and surely by now she doesn't care

about old secrets
and nothing I could say
would kill her anyway.

But I don't know any shamans,
so let's stick with the dream, Mom,
this Tuesday

or Wednesday, if that's better,
whenever works for you,
if you're busy I get it.

Daughter's Suitcase

She left almost as soon as she dragged in
her suitcase, only changed
and gone again.

There I sat with it
gaping. Boxing gloves,
a shed snakeskin,

books in some strange alphabet—whose?
Whose dress the color of mustard,
whose green spiked shoes?

I might have called the baggage office
but the jar of buttons—
that small pink heart, that tan leather knot—

and her braided hair in a plastic bag.
I smelled it for the smell of her,
faint, found

dirt in another bag
and in it, half unearthed, a small doll,
dirt where her teeth should be—

I pulled the pink plastic ring
from the hole in her neck,
heard only a long exhalation.

Late August Median

Today a faint rattle in the wind.
I leave town, drive the main road.
In the median, orange-vested men
shave lavender of its blooms, shape
each bush, an arrangement of green ottomans.
That sharp scent through the vents.
It takes me nowhere really.

Dream Car

How to get out, daughter, the car so precarious?
On your side, an ocean far below,
on mine, an outcrop of rock,
a barely survivable distance.
Why didn't you stop when I said stop?

Should we open both doors
to keep everything even?
Should we move fast or slow? If I jump out,
could you follow or would you
go down with the suddenly plunging car?

If I lean toward you, can you
creep to the console between us?
I could slowly close my door
to keep things even
as you crawl onto my lap.

I liked it better when I was the driver.

Will I always be in this car?

And why, on your side, the ocean?
Why, on mine, these rocks?

Life Still with Daughter

Whom I love. Ally
and antagonist. Who likewise
loathes sexism. Who loves me. Who laughs

at my ignorance. Who sings with me,
who goes silent. Who remembers my past
and present sins. Who points out everything

I lack. My categories out of date.
Who sees "woman" as a small box
and refuses to get in.

I stretch large to show there is room.
But bruise my head.
Who then kisses it, holds my hand,

tsk-tsks. Who will not make the bed.
Who needs a friend but gets a mother.
Who needs a mother but a better one.

Who demands I expand my heart and I do.
Who wants more than that: my mind
synced completely. Available, with no hovering.

Who is afraid. Who lives with pain
and persists. Who would rather not.
Who needs money. Who loves beauty

and points out small wonders:
fledgling owl in the undergrowth,
click of gravel under the foot of a snail.

Clam

Symmetrical sides
like an old Samsonite suitcase, once
a life tucked inside.
Salt wind
braids my hair like eelgrass. Tangled
dulse and bull kelp, washed up, buzzing flies.
How do their holdfasts fail?

The bulbous brown-green thick-skinned
air bladders, stepped on,
seep seawater, some kelpish smell.

I want to walk in a forest of kelp.
Green ribbon blades
would wave in slow motion.
Under the waves
I'd walk in slow motion.

Would I find you in the shade
of those gently bending stems?

Soothing, soothing,
the reliable tide,
the sea's distance
always temporary.

Casting Off

1

The dark green gap between
                          your boat, rocking
and the weathering dock

                    shifting, shifting
                    the elements

                    the green water, its anxious fishes
                    its lower shadows
                    now around you
not arranged to one side

oh, this push and pull, daughter
                          this drift

even the continents
                    wander

2

You face your leaving

        you navigate from that point

        only glimpses, the future
        over your shoulder

        occasional small
        adjustments

Your fists thrust toward what you left
        then lift

        leverage the blades into water behind you

        You pull the oars to push the water
        the water, reciprocal,
        shoves you back
        slap, slap, the sea against your hull

slap, slap, the same sea on the shore

Each Creature Holds On

Same going down dusk,
the hours enough
and the night certainly.

Needed now,
all leaf gold, marigold,
mustard. If my mother

had dared speak, I might
be visible. Silence
a hinterland

snare. Its
prickered vines
hold one so still.

All I Wanted

It caught and smashed the sound of me like silage—that wailing rain,
remembering the river and throwing itself down to her, upset-
ting the surface or impeded by a million needles and leaves,
mossed roof and gutters, gravel, grass blades, clay. Good-for-
nothing, all my shouting. All I wanted to know was
what stood between us. And all I wanted to know
was what stood between us.

The Real Daughter

And the daughter returns, ill, laid low.
And the mother makes up a bed for her.
And the mother feeds her three meals a day.

Each day the daughter cries.
Each day the mother holds her.
Each night the mother cries.

The daughter hopes for a different life.
The mother hopes for
the daughter she hoped for.

Of course she knows it's a fantasy.
Of course she loves the one she has.
Of course she misses the other one.

Something Good

For here you are, standing there, loving me,
Whether or not you should,
So somewhere in my youth or childhood,
I must have done something good.

OSCAR HAMMERSTEIN II

It's the song that soured *The Sound of Music*
for my grandfather, who long ago lobbed mud balls
at the kids in the Catholic schoolyard
adjacent to his Calvinist one. Total Depravity,
both precept and praxis, proved
even a moment of childhood goodness
earned you nothing. But my mother
bought the record and I learned it,
and this song, the most papist of the lot, is the one
I keep humming since my daughter came home.

I blamed myself when she left,
though the Calvinist God's supposed to
have it all predestined anyway, but that
"Train up a child in the way he should go" verse
no doubt tripped me up repeatedly. Had to stop believing
it was so simple.

As for my youth or childhood,
it's true I was known as a good girl
until I took up dancing. But only when
I loved did I believe myself good.
Yet surely other mothers have loved better than I
and have lost children they loved.
Of course, the song is ridiculous.

But in the movie, in the dark gazebo,
Maria in her floaty blue dress
and the captain in his tuxedo,
they don't really believe it either, the song,
nor their good luck, and like them,
I am incredulous about mine, and hope
there's something good I can't remember
that will secure it.

That Jettison Tactic

You know that jettison tactic—that dropping of pots and pans
you decide, after all, to do without,

that shedding of the heavy coat,
lightening yourself and your load,

because who knew the road would be this rough,
your body this tired?

There are people I would leave behind,
their care too much to carry.

But now, cold, I want my coat.
Hungry, I need my pots and pans.

The Tallest Thing

I have left the mountains. The trees also.
I am, here, the tallest thing.

And to the stars I've known in small clearings
are added all these who were formerly hidden,
the entire dome of them speaking from past ages.

I have yet to learn their names nor know how to introduce myself.
But I have taken with me my voice.

Or, I have taken my grandmother's voice.
Famke. Famke. Little girl. Little girl.

I have never been so visible.

May I sing your psalms, Grandmother,
to soothe myself?

May I sing them skeptical,
with a foreign tongue?

Follow-up Question

Grow up, I tell myself, let your grief simmer down to proper sadness—
you know you can't have what you want.

I want my dead mother
to teach me how to love my daughter.

Before I was born, she fed her, the egg within the egg.
As I was fed by my grandmother—

more cabbage, less meat,
the rough rye bread of wartime,

on Sundays half an egg.
Not enough for any of us

and now it's too late for follow-up questions,
like how on earth does a woman live.

From a Hollow

From a hollow, almost a hole,
the toad's ratcheted voice stops me.

There, the bumps of its eyes, its head
barely above the brown leaves.

Just a year ago, the phone call early.
I drove three hours, and my mother's face

cold. Someone had closed her eyes.
But her chest, under the covers, was still warm.

I can't get close or the toad will dive under.
The sounds it makes—

a tight throat?
Some resistance to the lungs?

We used to listen for the Swainson's thrush,
its lifting, liquid evensong.

This toad says only
            Here.

Acknowledgments

Thanks to the following journals for previous publication:

Compose: A Journal of Simply Good Writing   "And After" and "Marcescence"

Driftwood Press   "From a Hollow"

Eyedrum Periodically   "Maytag," "We Move to Morton Street," and "Comfort, Comfort Me"

Hartskill Review   "Makeup (for Three Faces)," here revised as "Makeup (The Mother, the Daughter, and the Other Daughter Speak)," and "Instructions for Interruptive Insomnia," also revised

Iron Horse Literary Review   "After the Flood"

Rascal   "Reading Wendell Berry to My Parents in the Hospital, *That Distant Land* Comes Close"

Raleigh Review   "Still with My Mother"

Right Hand Pointing   "By"

Sequestrum   "The Douglas Fir Leans Toward the House and I Pretend It Doesn't," "Dry Dock," and "Yoked"

Slipstream   "Four Parts Holy Water"

Strong Verse   "In This Green Green So Blue" and "French Kiss"

Young Ravens Review   "Piece of Knitting Pantoum"

Thanks to the National Humanities Center for supporting this work with a nine-month associate residency, providing a lovely place to work, excellent library support, and new friends. Thanks also to the Collegeville Institute for a one-week writing fellowship; St. David of Wales Episcopal Church for a summer writing residency, funded by a Lilly Endowment grant; and Portland State University for the Excellence Fellowship in Poetry.

Many people have helped me on the way to this book: friends and writing partners Stephanie C. Smith and Lisa Ohlen Harris; early manuscript readers Debby Jo Blank, Ralph Earle, Ashley Harris, Maura High, William Jolliff, Richard Krawiec, and David Mehler; my MFA advisor Michele Glazer, who provided feedback on many iterations of this book, and who, along with John Beer, Joanna Klink, and Michael McGregor, ensured the time I spent pursuing a formal education in writing was exhilarating and liberating; my poetry cohort at Portland State University and members of the Hornet Court, Black Socks, and Morton Street critique groups; Julie Funderburk, who served as Unicorn Press's First Book Award judge in 2017; and Unicorn Press editor Andrew Saulters. I am also grateful the encouragement I received from my sisters, my children, and especially my husband, Paul Otto, as I found my way.

Lynn Otto is a freelance academic copy editor and writing mentor. She holds an MFA from Portland State University, was a 2015/16 resident associate at the National Humanities Center, and now lives in Oregon.

Text and titles in Fournier.
Section numbers in Centennial.
Cover and interior design
by Andrew Saulters.

The author signed 26 hardbound copies,
lettered A through Z. An additional 75
hardbound copies and 400 bound in paper
were produced by Unicorn Press.

Titles in the Unicorn Press First Book Series

FIRST BOOK AWARD

Real Daughter by Lynn Otto
Celadon by Ian Haight
Self-Portrait in Dystopian Landscape by Stephen Lackaye
Winter Inlet by Hastings Hensel
Earthquake Owner's Manual by Martin Arnold

EDITOR'S CHOICE

Antipsalm by Wayne Johns
Remake by Colleen Abel
California Winter League by Chiyuma Elliott